Mommy remember me its your Daughter

My journey as a Caregiver

Denise Sinkfield

Copyright © 2016 by Denise Sinkfield

Mommy remember me its your Daughter
My journey as a Caregiver
by Denise Sinkfield

Printed in the United States of America.

ISBN 9781498467001

All rights reserved solely by the author. The author guarantees all contents are original and do not infringe upon the legal rights of any other person or work. No part of this book may be reproduced in any form without the permission of the author. The views expressed in this book are not necessarily those of the publisher.

Unless otherwise indicated, Scripture quotations taken from The Holy Bible, New International Version (NIV). Copyright © 1973, 1978, 1984, 2011 by Biblica, Inc.™. Used by permission. All rights reserved.

www.xulonpress.com

Dedication

This book is dedicated to my children George, Christopher, & Courtney for your love and encouragement, to my sister Pat for your strength, wisdom, and confidence, to my niece LaToya for your courage and inspiration, to my husband Tony for never letting me give up and loving me in spite of my faults, and finally to my Mother who is my hero.
Thank you all for inspiring me to reach beyond the stars
and believing in me when I didn't believe in myself.

I LOVE YOU ALL

Acknowledgements

All praises and thanks belong to God for allowing me to tell my story and never letting go of me during this difficult journey.

There aren't enough words in the universe to truly express how much gratitude and love I have within my heart for you my Lord. A big thank you to all my friends and family for encouraging me to see beyond the pain and giving me tough love especially when I wanted to throw in the towel. I am forever grateful to my three sons for believing in me even when I didn't believe in myself and for loving me in spite of my flaws. Your struggles and triumphs have given me the strength and courage to continue being the best that I can be. I truly appreciate my husband and my niece for motivating me to never give up and giving me words of wisdom that made the journey much easier to bear and for that you will always have my heart. I couldn't have made this journey without my sister and it's because of her love, ambition, and drive I was able to stand when I wanted to fall. Your encouraging words of wisdom always lifted me up especially when I was discouraged and depressed, and for that I will forever be grateful. I love you beyond words, and I thank God everyday for allowing me to be your sister. Thank you all from the bottom of heart because this journey would not have been possible without all of you.

About the Author

I was born and raised in New Rochelle, NY on September 26, 1956 to the late Leroy & Josie Manuel. I am the oldest of 3 siblings and I always enjoyed my younger years growing up in the housing projects of Hartley Houses. Throughout my early years I always knew I would write a book about someone or something that impacted my life and little did I know it would be a journey of heartaches, triumphs, mishaps, and joy. I am happily married for 9 years to my wonderful husband Tony and my greatest accomplishments are my three sons George, Christopher, and Courtney. I am the proud grandmother of 4 grandchildren Linise, Breana, Jamir, and Austin which was the best gift's given to me by God. My life has had many rewarding moments and I've had my share of sorrows and failures but there is one thing I do know and that is my failures have made me who I am today humble self confident and secure. I am a child of God who is still under construction and I hope that my journey will encourage others to hold on and never give up even if the road is rocky and narrow. Love is the greatest gift God gave to us and with love we can conquer the world.

Always be humble and true to yourself because it is the one thing that makes us who we are and defines our character as Human Beings.

Table of Contents

Dedication iii
Acknowledgments v
About the Author vii
Introduction xi
Chapter 1: The morning my Life
                 Changed Forever 13
Chapter 2: New Beginnings 20
Chapter 3: Feeling like a Damsel
                 in Distress 26
Chapter 4: Staying Encouraged 37
Chapter 5: Trying to Understand 45
Chapter 6: No Song in my Heart 52
Chapter 7: God Please Take the Wheel 60
Chapter 8: Losing Faith 72
Chapter 9: Desperately Seeking Help 78
Chapter 10: The Journey ends 85

Introduction

Caring for my mother afflicted with Alzheimer's was one of the most difficult things I never had to do in my life. The challenges associated with Alzheimer's left me feeling depressed, empty, angry, confused, and sad. It was a journey that brought about emotions I never knew existed which sometimes had me feeling as if I wanted to throw in the towel. This is a detailed account of my 12 years as a caregiver. My intention for you is to understand that it takes courage, patience, love, faith and understanding to care for a loved one afflicted by this horrible disease. The road will not be easy but the tribulations you face will give you strength you never even knew you had. I stayed on course with God's help and I want Caregivers to know in order to survive you will need support of family and friends, prayer, and a sense of humor. No matter how difficult it gets for you, as a Caregiver you must remember they are scared, confused, hostile, and frail. My journey helped me to realize that the ingredients needed for this recipe was love and patience. The disease leaves you feeling heartbroken but in the end, love and God will get you through the storm. My message for you simply is to remember that the person you are caring for once cared for you. They need all the love, kindness, and understanding you can give which helped me through this long and difficult journey.

Chapter 1

The morning my Life Changed Forever

I was expecting it to be an ordinary Sunday morning as I prepared for fellowship with the covenant disciples of Bethesda Baptist Church, but little did I know that it would turn out to be a morning that would change my life forever. My mother who was always full of life, the caregiver, the dreamer, and a woman who loved the Lord seemed confused and distant. Conversations were short and repetitive, and my mother's attention to detail and long talks were diminishing right before my eyes. I started to witness a change that I could not explain in my mother's appearance and vocabulary that had me baffled. The sunshine that once prevailed when she entered a room was now a cloud that was dark where she sat as I watched trying to understand the confusion I was feeling. The image that stood tall and confident a week ago was now an image that was frail and uncertain. It pierced my heart as I watched the rose wilting quickly before my eyes. I struggled to make sense of what was happening to the woman I always called upon for advice and comfort. I knew that my mother's world somehow appeared to be at a standstill and yet I could not figure out why. Feeling brokenhearted, I left the congregation in a state of panic to beckon my baby sister. Upon speaking with my sister, we both agreed that our mother's conversations were definitely repetitive and it was time to seek an expert opinion. We met at her house after church and my sister confirmed her demeanor was fragile and her state of mind seemed a little out of the ordinary. It was obvious to both of us that something was wrong and we needed to find out what was causing our mother to be so distant from her surroundings. My mother had always been an adventurer doing whatever her carefree spirit desired with her friends. Then suddenly she became a loner who just wanted to go to church and occupy a space on the bench to observe people passing by in front of her building. Little did my sister, and I know that the following months would change our lives forever. The bible says that we are to honor thy mother and thy father (Exodus20:12) but because my mother and I had a rather unusual relationship I was not trying to focus on the Christian way. In my mind, I wanted my mother to be her normal self so I would not have to be responsible for being her caregiver. I pushed my way through the negative electricity that was rushing through my body so I could come together as a team with my sister for the sake of my mother's well-being. My sister's love and God's strength reminded me of the nurturing my mother gave unselfishly. The journey began as my sister and I made plans, scheduled appointments, and rearranged my mother's world while we tried to keep her comfortable. Frustrated and confused I pulled my energy from my sister as we searched for new a doctor. Upon finding a doctor, we heard the unexpected answer to all our questions regarding my mother's appearance. The repetition and the sudden mood swings seemed to make sense as the doctor explained the symptoms of Alzheimer's disease. My mother was able to function on her own but it was apparent that her memory was decreasing. The things that she once knew how to do were difficult and confusing to accomplish. My sister and I now had to begin the process of elimination by attempting to move my mother out of her environment for safety reasons. Her resistance was so forceful we decided to seek professional support for some guidance. My mother was becoming bitter towards my sister and I and we had no clue why. Who was this person attacking us with such an angry disposition? After careful research and countless conversations with her doctor, it was clear to us that her unpredictable mood swings were normal. Changing the environment can only cause confusion and frustration in the mind of someone afflicted with this disease. So the decision was to let my mother stay where she was familiar. She made it perfectly clear to us that she was not moving no matter what we said. All I could remember thinking was this is to stressful specially since my world was already spinning like a tornado. I was not willing to accept the diagnosis so I began to block it out of my mind. Feeling disconnected I had to humble myself move back home and take on the title of "Caregiver". It took a while for me to understand why moving back to the place I left so many years ago would benefit my mother. My mother was unable to perform everyday living tasks that were essential for surviving without supervision. Cooking, cleaning, washing, and personal hygiene were difficult to accomplish. My full-time job description changed and a new set of rules were set in place. I now had the task of making breakfast for my mother, which for me was outdated since my children were adults. It was difficult making meals for someone whose demeanor was hostile and uncooperative. I was frustrated and angry since I did not want to be there in the first place. My mother did not want a babysitter because in her mind she had everything under control. It took all my power not to lose control and lash out at her. I did not have to take the abuse, and frankly, I just wanted to throw in the towel and let her take care of herself. I knew her loss of memory would make that impossible so I cried many nights and days. The pain, the pressure, and the responsibility were more than I wanted or thought I could handle at the time. Returning home for me was like a nightmare but a blessing for my mother. I was beginning to experience low self-esteem returning to the house where I always felt isolated and unsociable. I tried to understand it was the disease but my attitude spiraled while my mental state wandered towards isolation. I needed to escape the trauma that had inflicted my body, mind, and soul. In those 6 months, I became the reluctant caregiver as my mother's disease progressed and her mood swings increased. A life that was already flustered was now upside down. It became a life of chaos, confusion, resentment, and sadness for the daughter who was in denial.

Caring for someone with Alzheimer's takes away your joy and leaves you feeling miserable and depressed. My mother was confused and despite all the negative electrons that were racing in my body I tried to care for her with all my love. I was angry because I was losing her to the disease and our arguments reminded me of our wounded relationship as mother and daughter. In my mother's mind, I was the defiant child, and I needed her to see the responsible, strong, and independent woman I was trying to become. We were on one accord as mother and daughter for a brief moment before the disease took control. I sought to make a conscious effort to let go of resentful feelings from the past so I could communicate in my mother's world. What was I to do since I needed the future to exist in her mind? It was a tear-jerking long 6 months but my breakthrough had finally arrived.

Chapter 2

New Beginnings

I was elated with joy and sad at the same time because I was not sure if the time was right to move. All I knew was that I could not continue on this path of destruction. I was now a "Caregiver" from the comforts of my home which made me so happy. Now my sister and I had to begin thinking about specific care for our mother which changed our lives. The process of moving her from the environment she had known for 50+ years caused problems far beyond our imagination. My mother of course was defiant but my sister and I moved her in spite of her complaints. In our opinion it was the best thing for her well-being but here I was again in a place that felt uncomfortable which was being a "Caregiver". I pulled energy from my sister so I could focus on what was best for my mother. I was still in denial and all I wanted was for her mind to return to the future. So I blocked out the evitable and chose to indulge in anger rather than understand the circumstances. The move began which was difficult and challenging for my sister and me since my mother kept going back to her old environment. We had disturbed her world and rearranged her comfort zone which made her completely confused. Alzheimer's is such a baffling disease that you never know your opponents next move. My sister and I wrestled with my mother for one year and she was finally familiar with her new surroundings. Now that my mother had adjusted to her new surroundings we were able to pick up where we left off in our own our lives. The telephone was a means of communication during the day which eased my mind while at work. I was thankful that the disease had not wiped out the memory of being able to answer the phone from my mother's mind. The calls helped in guiding her to the refrigerator for meals that were prepared the night before. It was mandatory for us to make sure she was eating until we arrived from work. I was not however convinced since we were not actually there to watch her eat. We needed a physical body present for reassurance but this method had to suffice for now. During this process I witnessed my mother's hostility soaring to a high latitude and I was on the verge of a nervous breakdown. Her mood swings were like thorns piercing my heart and mind as she became more confrontational and rebellious. My mother told us she was the mother and what right did we have telling her how to live her life. We had no clue what to do but we both knew something had to be done. At this point I wanted to disappear and never return because this scenario was to much to handle. My mother's abusive behavior was unacceptable and something had to be done in a hurry because the volcano was about to erupt.

I had my own life and family to think about and I surely wanted no parts of her temperament. It was the love I had for my mother and my religion that allowed me to step outside the box. It was obvious she realized something was happening that she could not explain which always triggered the gun towards us. My mother became angry, frustrated, confused, and scared because she did not know how to express the anguish she was feeling. I needed to put aside my feelings and help find a solution to bring back the sunshine that was diminishing in my mother's world. My sister and I began to pray as we put all our trust in God to help us find a solution to the problem. We were at our wits end and aggravation was becoming inescapable as we searched for answers concerning our mother. We did however agree that we would do everything in our power to keep her out of a nursing home. Caring for a loved one with Alzheimer's requires two essential ingredients. Patience and support something I did not feel within my heart. My soul was already in a state of turmoil and the ingredients needed to survive this ordeal had a bitter taste in my mouth. My mother was becoming challenging to manage and I was trying fervently to keep an open mind. I prayed for an answer to my predicament because I did not know how much longer I could bear the agony. I wanted to take a trip to a land far away where there was peace and tranquility. I needed someone to rescue me from the demons that were running through my mind. In the midst of my resentment, God sent an answer by way of a conversation between my sister and her hairstylists. He offered a solution to our problem because his father had the same temperament as my mother. He suggested talking to the doctor about giving her medicine to calm her moods which helped him cope with his father. The mood swings were spiraling out of control and she seemed depressed, but I still did not want to deal with the issue. We presented our case to the doctor hoping for a solution to our problem. He agreed her behavior was unstable and advised that she be medically evaluation before prescribing any medication. We needed to identify what was triggering the behavior which was important in determining what antidepressant he would give our mother. It was confirmed that my mother was suffering from depression which explained her mood swings. The antidepressant much to our surprise was the best thing to happen to us. We were amazed how my mother's conversations went from being abusive to becoming friendly. I remember she would always say when we asked her to do something

"Whatever you say dear" which made me smile. My mother's attitude was now soothing to the soul but I still struggled with old wounds that had taken residency in my mind. My broken relationship with my mother from past experiences was still leaving a sour taste in my mouth. When the heart aches from resentment it is difficult to concentrate on being a loving caregiver. In spite of my negativity I needed to rise and soar like an eagle high above the clouds. My mother was receptive to our instructions regarding her care which allowed us to exhale for a moment as we continued our busy schedule.

Chapter 3

Feeling like a Damsel in Distress

*W*e juggled, maintained, and rearranged our lives according to the care and needs of our mother. Minimal supervision was efficient as long as the phone calls continued as a means of communicating during the day. We tried to keep her day from being complicated so she wouldn't feel frustrated. I had to once again humble myself to accommodate my mother as my sister and I alternated days. Our lives would never be the same but because of my profound love I rose above the pain in spite of my needs. Imagine for a moment if you will your parent wandering to an unknown place that even you cannot reach. It was as if glass had fallen and shattered into little pieces that I was unable to recover. I needed my mother's advice, support, discipline, and shoulder to cry on. Unfortunately, she was not capable of giving me the motherly attention I desperately needed. The reality of it all was just too much to bear and I wondered if I could ever recover from this horrible nightmare. I had no choice but to lift my head up high because I was so grateful just to have her in my presence. A mother's approval is every child's desire and I wanted to hear "I am so proud of you" which would never be music to my ears. Time had approached so rapidly and so did the diseases' progression that my sister and I realized we needed additional help. My mother needed to be in a program that offered services for individuals who were suffering from the same disease. Our mission was to keep my mother in the comforts of her home while searching for additional services. We needed a daytime program and someone to keep her house in order during the times we were at work. The thought of looking for additional help was too much to handle. I felt the burden of despair as I pondered the idea of someone else caring for my mother. I still didn't appreciate how my life was interrupted and it was a struggle every day to keep doing was right. It was not any fault of my mother that she had this baffling disease but I still was feeling emotionally disconnected from all the stress. I just wanted someone else to experience the agony I dealt with every minute and second of the day. I realized that my experiences were personal and unless someone walked in my shoes they could never imagine my pain. I just wanted the pain that was piercing my soul like thorns to move from my body to someone else's body. After countless hours of phone calls and visits, my sister found an adult day care program that was suited for my mother's needs. We went to observe a typical day at the program and we were pleasing surprised how the staff attended to everyone's needs with such care and concern. They offered activities that required the patients to function in an environment that was fitting for their individual needs. It was refreshing to know that opportunities were available that focused on motor and cognitive skills. I was elated knowing that the program provided activities which kept the mind busy even though it only retained the past. Several weeks went by and my mother seemed to be adapting to her new surroundings and friends at the program.

We saw a change in her attitude that was like a ray of sunshine glistening on the water which was simply breathtaking. The program and the additional help gave my sister and I a chance to relax for at least a couple of hours. It was something we had not experienced in a while and I welcomed the freedom with open arms. My mother's household was now in order which gave my sister and me a chance to put the scrambled pieces of our puzzled lives back together. Caregiver's are like doctors always on call to attend to the needs of loved ones' who are having difficult moments of forgetfulness, anxiety, anger, frustration, and depression. In order to make their lives comfortable you have to be willing to let go of your situation and feelings so you can give one hundred and one percent of your time. This kind of change can be difficult and almost impossible especially if your life is already on a roller coaster ride. I never imagined my mother not being able to remember or understand the simple things in life. Things like brushing her teeth, changing her clothes, taking a bath, or even recalling if you ate were erased from her mind. It was so hard to digest, but I pushed forward feeding off the energy of my sister and the comfort from God. My mother's disease kept deteriorating and it was difficult trying to find options to keep her safe. Each day for me was exhausting as the load on my back got heavier from the burden I carried. I was sinking like the titanic and there was no way out of the bottomless pit. My mother was now my child who needed nurturing and guidance because everything she once knew was completely unfamiliar. In the midst of the typhoon, my mother somehow knew something was not quite right. The difficulties associated with the disease made it challenging for her to communicate the change in her life.

The agony I faced watching my mother moving in a backwards motion was beginning to take a toll on me physically and mentally. I needed family support more than ever to hold my hand and comfort my aching heart. I wanted the strength of an ox along with a shoulder to lean on since the pain was too much to endure. In fact, God had to intercede on my behalf because without Him I would never be able to finish the journey. My sister and I encouraged each other when my mother's behavior became irrational and we leaned on God for guidance. We agreed to keep her in the comforts of her home as long as possible even if the journey was hectic. Months passed, years flew by, and the disease just kept sprinting as if it was running a 55-yard dash. Emptiness filled my heart the day my mother's memory of me being her daughter went away like the sun when it sets for the evening. The doctor warned us that the day would come when she would not remember we were her children, which crushed my heart. I cannot begin to express the devastation I felt deep within my soul that caused tears to flow like the waterfalls at Niagara Falls. "It's your daughter don't you know who I am" became a song that I sang every time I visited my mother.

There were times when my heart would race with joy at the sound of her recalling my name even if it was only for a split second. The enthusiasm I felt hearing her say Denise warmed my heart only to have the joy taken away like a thief who comes in the night. In my mother's world I went from being her daughter to becoming her friend. Oh, how I yearned for my mother to remember her oldest child which was inevitable since her mind was like a see saw going up and down. How was I to deal with the fact that the disease was robbing my mother of the present? I had to figure out a way to cope with the fact that her mind was like faucets hot one minute and cold the next. The past was all she was capable of giving me and I needed her to see the responsible caring woman I was becoming. The mother and daughter bond that we were building was now useless because she only could remember the defiant me who was a radical growing up. How do you get someone to remember the future when they are only capable of the remembering is the past? I never thought that a name and the future would have such an impact as it did when I realized my mother's mind was wilting away right before my eyes. I felt so alone and abandoned that I became a turtle hiding in my shell distant from the outside world and my family. I had to learn to put my emotions on the shelf and pick up my wounded heart so I could continue caring for our mother. It was not an easy task and I kept telling myself that my God would take on my burdens so I could have rest. I too was like the faucets and I chose to let my emotions of the past block my view of what God was speaking to my heart. All I knew was my mother was clueless who I was and for me I could not or did not want to understand why this was happening. Reality would soon let me know that it was not about my feelings but it was all about my mother who was the one that lost her memory. The pieces of the puzzle I was trying so desperately to piece back together would never tell a story or portray a picture because the pieces were lost forever. In my mind, I wanted God to make it go away so I could resume my life and my mother's world would be normal. Unfortunately, that did not happen so the journey continued and my mother minds played hide and go seek which was hard to reach. The disease expanded like a rubber band and caring for her was becoming more unbearable each day. I noticed my mother's actions were becoming physical and she began to attack her prey like the claws of a lion looking for food. She was becoming combative which made it tough at times to control her behavior. My mother's vocabulary penetrated the heart that I did not know she even knew such vulgar words. How was as it possible for a human being to talk to another human being in that matter especially to her daughters. It was hard to digest because I still was having a hard time trying to separate the fact the disease was the reason for the rowdy conduct. I once again tried to keep my head above water because I felt like I was about to drown in the sorrows of my broken heart. I dug deep into my soul and prayed every day for guidance to help me through the maze. It was imperative for me to be on one accord with my sister caring my mother in the midst of the battlefield.

I managed to weave and bob through the physical attacks but I could not find an escape behind the cruel words that gnawed at my self-esteem. The harsh words kept me from giving my undivided attention because flashbacks of the past kept reminding me of the bond I never had with my mother. There were endless nights of tears as I kept the agony within myself trying to be mindful that she needed my help. I realized that someone greater than myself was governing my thoughts as I recalled the nurturing my mother had given to me all my life. Just like the program, I had to nurture my mother with love and tender care. My mother's dilemma was so much more devastating than anything I was feeling, and I was still in a state of shock. I just wanted a little normality to return to my world.

Mommy remember me its your Daughter

Chapter 4

Staying Encouraged

I had days that were depressing and some that were awesome but through it all I tried to keep my mother carefree and happy. Our routine along with the program and the additional helped assured us her safety was in good hands. I felt like a tree transitioning into winter as the beautiful leaves begin to fall off making their appearance bare, which was how I visualized my world as a caregiver. My physical being and mental state felt like I was sinking in quick sand. The days seemed shorter and the nights seemed longer as I pressed through the weariness of dealing with my mother's roller coaster moods. It was so heartbreaking day in and day out watching someone who was so energetic and independent slowly disintegrating right before my eyes. The one good thing that made sense out of all the chaos was the day program that became my mother's home away from home. There was no need to worry about the safety of my mother during the day since the program provided the protection we were so anxiously seeking for her. My mother was now interacting with other patients who had the same difficulties trying to function in a world that was confusing. The program was instrumental in reinforcing activities to stimulate the brain. They focused on everyone being encouraged to complete tasks that seem impossible because of the disease. It was always a pleasure to visit the program as I watched my mother interact with the patients singing, dancing, and conversing with one another. There were times when she would become defiant but that never stopped the staff from finding ways for her to keep her mind constantly motivated. So for the moment things appeared to be normal considering the circumstances. I became a robot as I continued my daily routine of alternating care for my mother with no expectations. I was of tired of the vicissitudes that were associated with Alzheimer's as I tried to understand the many sagas of the disease. Resentment nestled within my soul because I refused to expunge those childhood memories that kept haunting my mind. Instead I allowed myself to imagine that my mother's mind was normal which was a false reality. I did not want to believe this disease had affected someone that I loved. There were times when I felt she knew something was not quite right and I was helpless because there was nothing I could do to make it go away. How do you to explain to a woman who was vibrant, outgoing, caring, and independent that her memory was drifting to an unknown place of no return? It was so hard to watch a loved one trying to cope with this disease and the only word I constantly found myself using was "Why". I needed answers and science had no cure or even an explanation for the sudden rise of the disease among the old and young. It was affecting the world at a brisk speed and I never in a million years would have thought it would affect my mother. Why was this happening to my mother and why was I feeling lonely and confused.

I really did not have time to concentrate on the reason because it was truly all about keeping my mother safe and secure. I was frustrated and angry because the woman I had looked up to all my life was now someone I didn't even recognize. I painfully realized there was nothing I could do to fix the problem so the only solution in my mind was to lash out at the ones I loved. I had to find a way to work through my emotions so I could continue nurturing my mother who needed my supervision. I focused on telling my mother how much I loved her as I embraced her with hugs and kisses. I knew it was a matter of time before the words and gestures would be a question mark in her mind. My mother was still able to talk walks, communicate even though it was repetitive and do daily routines under supervision which gave me hope. The goal was to let my mother perform everyday tasks on her own even it meant doing it at a slower pace. The ability to dress herself, brush her teeth, use the bathroom, and lock the apartment door were tasks we required her to achieve on her own. We did not want the disease to stumble her ability to continue using her motor and cognitive skills. I was glad when we sat outside eating ice cream and watching television even if it made no sense in her mind. It was a pleasure seeing her face light up with a smile as she savored the taste of ice cream melting in her mouth. Everything was going as well as expected that I almost forgot the disease had consumed my mother's mind. Some things are not what they appear to be with someone who has Alzheimer's and reality knocks your emotions down constantly. What appears to be signs of improvement are baffling for the caregiver especially when the person appears to be normal. The disease leaves you feeling confused and disappointed because just when you think there is a light at the end of the tunnel a fog appears and blurs your vision. Imagine if you will someone in a coma waking up for a moment then slipping back into the coma. That's how my mother's mind was functioning and it was a devastating feeling to watch as the door was slowly beginning to close on the present. It shattered all my hope of her mind ever returning to normal. Those were the times I asked myself why, and cried out in agony wondering what kind of cruel game was I suppose to be playing. I did not want to be tested by God at this point because I was not even sure if I had any faith. I was tired of being happy one minute and then sad the next minute. So I encouraged myself to keep my emotional state from becoming stale because it needed to be alive. Peace within my soul non existed since the storm was raging and I needed the boat to be still. I did everything in my power given to me by God to keep my mother nestled in her security blanket. I tried to give her all the love and support that was inside me even though my heart was aching. Alzheimer's is such a distorted disease that you have to be prepared mentally and physically for the many faces that it beholds. I watched my mother go from reality to confusion, confusion to withdrawal, and withdrawal to depression day in and out. There were however times when she appeared to know what was going on but most of the time she was confused.

The sunshine quickly turned into an eclipse that always left me feeling distant, confused, and lost. I believe that all things work to them that love the Lord yet I could not understand how this scripture related to my mother's present state. I wanted the Lord to bring her back from the darkness in her mind into the light that I saw shining at the end of the tunnel. The solemn journey continued and I kept hoping for a change even though I knew it was not realistic. It was hard to care for a loved one when deep within my soul a war was raging that caused chaos within my body. Determined to stand tall even when I was crumbling I focused all my energy towards the song that kept playing in my heart. I tried to sing but the melody just seemed to elude the passage way from my heart to my mouth. The song was buried deep inside the pain which had taken control of my thoughts. My mother was content in her world while my world on the other hand was complex and depressing with no signs of happiness. I attempted to focus on trying to stay positive because in all honesty I was about to explode. I could feel my emotions taking on rough waters as if I was white water rafting.

Chapter 5

Trying to Understand

*I*t is funny how now I missed the things in life that use to make me feel so emotionally disconnected growing up. I wished my mother would yell at me just one more time to straighten me out but that was just a figment of my imagination. Life's experiences are so unpredictable and even though my past with my mother was painful I truly wanted them back in my life. They may have been uncomfortable but I wanted back the mother I knew before the disease took control of her mind. Witnessing her in this state of withdrawal and uncertainty was overwhelming, heartbreaking, and confusing. I felt like a willow tree slumped over in depression for eternity with no chance of sprouting into a vibrant happy branch. The desire to visit her was becoming invisible since I wanted to run far away so I could escape the responsibilities of being a caregiver. The needs of my mother outweighed my needs so I pressed forward trying to control the situation. Evening walks, talks on the bench, and bedtime stories somehow gave me peace. Taking care of my mother had its difficulties which made it hard to know if my day would be rocky or smooth. So I continued to be the loving caregiver which I sometimes tried to elude. My mother finally had some contentment in her world for the moment and she appeared to be glistening like the moon over the sea. We wanted my mother's life to be peaceful and radiant like the sun that greets you in the morning with a smile. I felt she had endured enough darkness and confusion in such a short time that she needed a break. It was time for her to enjoy the beautiful surroundings of the birds chirping, people talking, children playing, and flowers blooming even if she had no clue who or what they were. It was sad to watch her struggling trying to accomplish a task that use to be so easy once upon a time.

My sister and I became the voices that guided my mother through the maze. I was still having a hard time with the whole situation even though I smiled through the pain when people asked how she was doing. My mother began to show signs of withdrawal that indicated the disease was moving faster than my sister and I could have predicted. Some days were more intense than others but the staff at the program never let her wander to far from the outside world. They kept her involved in activities that allowed her to focus on task so she would not gaze off into the sunset. I still often imagined that one day I would walk into the program and my mom would be her normal self. I wanted life to resume the way it used to be organized and carefree. I often dreamed I would hear her say in her motherly voice "Why the heck am I here in this place for old people I am not old"? A dream that would never come to pass because the mind does not recover it regresses. It was inevitable but my dreams were the only moments I had that gave me joy. I just wanted my mother back so we could pick up where we left off building our relationship. My aching heart needed a miracle that I knew would never happen.

Subsequently I held on to my dreams as I watched in agony my mother drifting further and further away from me. The world that consumed her mind was now memories of the past and the future did not exist. We designed a plan to protect my mother, but I had so many things to say and yet so many words were left unspoken between us. I finally found a place within my mother's heart before the demon called Alzheimer's shattered my dreams. My mother only remembered me as the defiant child and that made me miserable. The disease wins the battle over your conscious and if you are trying to build a torn relationship nothing in the present matters. I needed the past not to overpower the present because I wanted my mother to remember the relationship we were building instead of the one where we bumped heads. A mother's love next to God's love soothes the soul which brightens up your heart like a Christmas tree. We all yearn for love from our parents because it's the one thing that makes us feel special. I needed a celebration to take place within my heart but instead it was having a funeral. The funeral was burying the present and in my mind it needed to lay the past to rest. What was I to do except continuously pray for a miracle and hold my head up high. I became my mother's right and left arm, her voice, and her protector as I pushed my way through the storm trying to keep calm. The only way for me to stay focused was to channel my fears by writing my emotions on paper. I expressed how I felt whenever the disease would produce a character that was unlike my mother through words. When in distress it is always good to express your thoughts on paper which gave me peace and comforted my soul "I loved when she would greet me in the morning with a smile that warmed my heart when it was broken and quenched my thirst when I felt dry like the desert thoughts of her always cheered me up because her love besides God's was the one thing that never changed she always told me to reach for the stars and never give up on your dreams she is the joy, the laughter, and the strength when I am depressed I call her mom and her love means everything to me nothing or no disease will ever replace that love." No matter what my mind might be telling me I know that my mom's love will never leave me. I need to channel my love so I could give it back to her as her caregiver. Changes were about to surface in spite of the program being a safe haven for my mother. My mother's demeanor was rapidly spiraling into a new monster that I was not ready to challenge. The staff was patient and licensed to handle the altered character that began to show its ugly face. I was her daughter and I had no clue how to control my emotions that was becoming a problem again for me. Old demons would creep back in every time I would stumble upon unfamiliar territory when it came to mother's erratic behavior. It was so easy to let the demons that haunted my feelings from the past consume my thoughts. I always needed an excuse to focus on the past instead of trying to handle what was going on in the present. I did not have the strength of an ox like my sister and I really did not want to be a caregiver.

In my mind, I never imagined we would have to do this all over again since dementia had stricken my Grandmother. Why was this similar situation happening because I had no desire to contribute any of my time then and I had none now? I needed everything to be normal since change for me was not part of my vocabulary now or ever. It was time for us to consider other options since my mother was developing unpredictable behavior associated with the disease. We needed more ammunition to control the army that was raging within my mother's mind and I wanted the present which was better for me. So I pulled myself together as we meditated on what the next step would be towards keeping my mother safe.

Chapter 6

No Song in my Heart

My sister reached out to my mother's medical advocate on obtaining a caregiver overnight which was the logical solution to my mother's dilemma. It wasn't as easy to obtain the overnight service as we thought since there were so many rules and regulations. Patients were required to pass a series of test before they would even be considered qualified candidates. In my mind, my mother needed the additional service and I really did not care about the rules or regulations. A nursing home was not an option even though the advocate suggested it might be something to carefully consider if denied the overnight service. I became frustrated, disappointed, anger, and sad upon hearing the news. So I immediately removed myself mentally and let my sister handle the situation because after all she was my mother's legal guardian. I gave my opinion when asked but whatever decision my sister deemed for my mother's care was fine with me. I did not even want or desired to have the responsibility of making the final choice. Specific processes had to take place and sometimes the explanations given just did not make any sense. It made me feel like they had no clue how severe my mother's condition was or if they even cared. I knew they were just doing their jobs but I was frustrated as I tried to understand their viewpoints. My mother needed a protector at night and her physical appearance made it seem like she was capable of taking care of herself. It was hard for my sister to plead her case because according to the advocate my mother appeared to be perfectly normal. This uncomfortable saga of feeling like I was on a see saw ride continued for months as my sister never gave up the fight for overnight service. In the mean time we had to once again re- arrange our schedules to become night watchmen to ensure my mother's safety. Why did I have to go through this wind tunnel again especially when I did not want to be involved in the first place? Whenever it was my time to be the night watchman I would develop an attitude that was quite disappointing. The bitterness that I encountered within my soul was very disturbing and ugly. The disease was beginning to take on a new shape and it was difficult to keep my mother balanced. She was starting to be quite inquisitive as children often do when they are on a quest to explore the environment in which they live. My mother began a transformation of her household which was obvious whenever I came to visit. You could see signs of destruction that made it seem like the apartment had been ransacked by robbers. The only difference was my mother was the intruder in her own home searching for anything that she thought in her mind existed. Her dresser draws, her nightstand, and the linen closet were the points of attack in my mother's plan of destruction. No matter how many times I tried to keep them in order she always made a mess. So my compulsive disorder of having things in order ceased within my mother's household. The sad part of this ordeal was that at one time she also shared the same compulsive disorder.

In my mother's mind the mess she was causing within her house was neat. Life can be complicated and adventurous but this voyage was not in my plan, and it needed to dissolve like ice from the sunrays. I witnessed once again the effects of the disease but I was at peace because my mother was not hurting herself or anyone. All she was doing was making a mess which actually was good because it meant she was still using her motor skills. It was funny sometimes when I would go to her house and see the masterpieces she would create from rearranging the clothes in the dresser draw which was very imaginative. I realized that the mind of someone with Alzheimer's is unique because even though they live in the past they are imaginative. My mother was not the adventurous type and she never took chances but the disease brought about a person who was assertive, daring, and confident. The only thing I still desired was for my mother to remember who I was. Every now and then she did but most of the time I was the invisible daughter which for me was crazy. My emotional state needed to be uplifted to a peaceful place so I kept trying to invent ways to ease the pain that kept piercing at my heart. You have no idea what it feels like to have a conversation with your mother that only included two or three words that ended with yes, no, or whatever you say. Spring and summer were the brighter seasons of my life whereas fall and winter were cool and brisk. The winter months kept me confined within my mother's walls where silence was the dominant factor between us. At least we could savor the sweet aroma of summer from the flowers as they began to blossom. As I watched my mother smile at the people passing in the distance I pondered how I would hold on since it felt like I was falling off a cliff. I was trying desperately to fight my way out of the maze which to me was never ending. My mother in my eyes was an alien and I could not imagine how she saw me now that she was afflicted with this disease. I recall one day when my mother was being rebellious she lashed out at me uttering I am going to tell my daughter. I looked at her completely puzzled because it was obvious I was a stranger and then I began to cry. I became withdrawn as I tried to understand that

I too might be an alien in her eyes. There was still no word for someone to come in at night and my frustration and resentment took on another level of anger and disappointment. My mind transformed into alters- egos much like those similar to the characteristics of Dr. Jekyll & Mr. Hyde. In was in those moments of transformation that I became very bitter towards the situation that caused me to lash out at anyone who was in my path. I secluded myself from the world outside and delved into a world of loneliness I created within which keep me numb and invisible to my surroundings. I wondered what kind of person was I becoming and was it even possible to change because I really didn't like myself. It was an ugly situation that bothered me and I did not know how to stop the pain. The sun needed to shine within my soul and I could not find the light at the end of this tunnel which was dark, gloomy, depressing, and scary.

Psalm 23 helped me to understand the way God protects his sheep I need to protect my mom even if the situation seems dim. I was her leader since she could no longer lead herself. It is amazing how God takes a situation which appears to be unfair and turns it around to be positive energy. The greatest reward for this situation was love which I unconditionally had for my mother. I was just having a hard time accepting the reality of the situation which was causing me to become a monster that I didn't even like. So here I was again trying to push pass the resentment so I could concentrate on my mother's needs and not mine.

Chapter 7

God Please Take the Wheel

As I patiently waited for the call to come in regarding the overnight caregiver I continued on my quest to keep my mother comfortable as I shared the tasks with my sister. I never thought in a million year my mother's life would be this twisted. I thought she would gracefully transition in becoming a senior citizen. There is no preparation for someone who has Alzheimer since it appears unexpectedly at any moment and attacks any age. I continued to seek guidance from God and close personal relationships in order to remain sane through the madness that was raging a war within my heart. God always showed me that in the midst of a storm there is peace and I found my peace on Sunday mornings preparing my mother for church service. Those times were special because the smile I witnessed on her face as she got dressed made everything seem irrelevant. My mother's world was a ball of confusion but somehow fellowship with the covenant disciples of Bethesda Baptist Church brought happiness to our world. Watching her explode with joy as the members greeted her was the tranquility I yearned for within my heart. As I listened to my mother sing the hymns, tap her feet, and clap her hands I knew in that moment the disease had not completely taken control of her mind. It was priceless and it was in church where I realized how I could communicate with my mother. Playing gospel music from my phone helped me to handle the impossible days as I attended to my mother's needs. It was the one thing besides sweets that kept her calm whenever she began to be unruly. The desire to get up and get ready for church was becoming difficult especially when all she wanted to do was sleep. I realized that my mother was waking up during the wee hours of the morning creating a mess which explained why she was so tired. The fact that she was getting up began to worry us and we desperately needed the approval for the weekend caregiver to happen. We needed to take precautionary measures so we removed the knobs off the stove, the kitchen knives, and had the gas turned off to ensure her safety. The approval was finally confirmed for the weekend and we were still able to keep the regularly scheduled caregiver during the week. My sister and I of course would still have to rotate bedtime hours during the week just to confirm she was safely tucked in for the night. I was still reluctant because of her waking up and I had to rely on my faith and believe that God would protect her until morning. The time that was divided between four capable individuals was truly a blessing and it helped me maintain my sanity. It took some time for my mother to adjust to her sleepover guest but she finally was receptive to the idea. She would have occasional outbursts and threaten the help but she never complained because my mother was her top priority. Months went by and I could see changes in the progression of the disease that had me on edge. I was however grateful for the caregiver's thoughtfulness to my mother's needs and household.

My mother always seemed pleasant when she had to interact with the caregiver which was a plus since she could be devious at unexpected times. I could still sense my mother was starting to wander to a place in her mind which kept her isolated from the outside world. She began to withdraw from us and any communication with other people. Sleep for her was now in the same category as a newborn because to her night was day and day was night. The nights became a nightmare for the caregiver on the weekends and impossible for me to handle during the week. We gave up our lives so that our mother would have a life that was carefree and safe but her sporadic behavior was causing fiction within my soul. I felt my efforts slowly melting away as I began to ponder was everything we did enough to keep my mother safe. She had taken on a new adventure which now was becoming impossible to handle even with all the woman power we had on guard. I was tired and mentally drained and I did not want the words nursing home to surface from beneath my pain. In my mind I knew that was the only solution to that would keep her safe and sound. We had exhausted all options possible and it was now time to have a family discussion that I did not want. I felt like the earth was a gigantic pillow suffocating me as I gasped for air trying to breathe. My mind skipped from east to west as decisions had to be made regarding my mother's safety which was becoming to difficult to even envision. So I conquered the inevitable and sat down with my sister as we evaluated our options regarding a safe haven for my mother. The search for nursing homes was long and exhausting which made the journey difficult to bear. While I dreaded the thought of her in a place where sometimes the care is not acceptable I had to be strong and put my mother's needs first. I heard and read so many bad stories about nursing homes that I was already skeptical about them caring for my mother. There honestly was not any nursing home in this world that I considered qualified enough to pass the test. I was scared not for my mother but for what I might do if those stories I read became a reality. My sister and I had done everything possible for my mother and it was time to let go and let God guide us in choosing the best home. There was nothing more that we could do since we had exhausted all the necessary measures in our power to keep her safe. My mother was becoming a menace to herself and to the caregivers that protected her at night. You cannot imagine what my sister and I were feeling because after all this was our mother who was still young and healthy. Her physical appearance did not exactly fit the profile of someone afflicted with this disturbing disease. She was a tall fashionable diva who was vibrant, sassy, and always greeted you with a smile and plenty of hugs. It was only evident that she was suffering from Alzheimer's when you would try to chat with her. Sunny days were gloomy and a cloud of darkness overshadowed me as I attempted to keep my focus on the task at hand.

It never dawned on me how many senior citizens were affected by this demon until we started searching for a nursing home. Conquering this task was much harder to grasp because there was so much pain I was experiencing within my soul. How could this possibly be that we were looking for nursing homes? My mother was to young and the possibilities of placing her in a nursing home was not in the cards at least not now so I thought. In my mind my mother was suppose to be outgoing, daring, loving, and healthy well into her 80's and I was not prepared to place her in a nursing home just yet. So I was not prepared and I don't know if any of us are ever prepared. I needed my mother and not this person who slipped away to an unknown place where only memories of the past lived in her mind. This was the hardest thing by far I ever had to do and frankly for the first time I forgot about our past relationship. I wanted to protect my mother guide and shelter her which I felt would slip away once she entered into a nursing home. My sister and I had provided a safe haven for her and I allowed myself not to feel any emotional attachments until now. I did what was needed to be done because she was my mother and I did not want my sister to carry the burden all by herself. Now the tables were turning and my emotions seemed to be shifting in a direction different that had me baffled. The emotions were always there I just suppressed them deep within so I would not have to feel. Now my back was against the wall because caring for my mother would now be in the hands of a nursing home. The thought of my mother living the rest of her life in a place other than her home was scary. I started to experience symptoms associated with asthma as I tried to gasp for air. The only thing left to do was to make sure that my mother would be comfortable no matter where her place of residency would end up being. We continued on our quest to find a suitable nursing home which at times was aggravating because all the prominent ones had long waiting lists. The journey was bumpy and it felt like a head on collision every time the possibilities of placing her in a facility crashed because of the wait. The process needed to occur like tomorrow and the headlights leading to a solution was becoming dimmer as we pressed forward. I wondered during the process if we would ever find a place since I had reservations about the care given to patients in nursing homes. My sister had the painful task of filling out applications and scheduling appointments as we prayed for someone to call with good news. As it transitioned from spring to summer our mission remained the same which was to keep my mother out of harm's way. Our lives were focused on my mother's world which was slowly becoming invisible in her mind. We were the only reason she could function from the disease which made her world confusing. A world that was full of excitement, happiness, spirituality, and giving quickly melted away like the witch in the Wizard of Oz right before my very eyes. The land that was once filled with an abundance of opportunities and adventures was now a land of confusion, resentment, and despair in my mother's mind.

I tried to erase the darkness that unveiled in her mind from the misfortune of the disease. Spring gracefully made an exist and summer eased its way in as we took one day at time hoping to hear something good about a nursing home. My mother was becoming more defiant making it difficult for us to handle her mood swings. Finally, a bed became available in a place that we least expected but was recommended by the daycare program. We made an appointment to consult with the director but in my mind the conversation should not be taking place. My sister and I were familiar with the facility and the director explained in detail the services that were available for Alzheimer patients. We were both satisfied with the results so the transformation of moving my mother to her new residency took place. I must admit during this time I was not happy and sadness consumed my body even though I knew we were doing the right thing for my mother. My sister's strength during this whole ordeal was electrifying and I often wondered how could she be so calm while I was a total wreck. During the process of relocating my mood was dismissive as the reality of the situation agitated my heart. It was obvious that she would not need much except the basic essentials, and frankly, I wanted her to remain in the place that she called home instead of the nursing home. We really had no other alternative because for 8 years we kept her happy and protected but she needed professional attention. The idea of placing her in the unknown made my heart shatter because the change was to much to handle. The nursing home appeared to be competent to handle the patients but I wondered if the staff was capable of dealing with my mother whose behavior was sometimes like a bull. There was no time to question their qualifications since it was crucial for my mother to have round the clock supervision. All we could do was pray and hope that everything would work in her favor which is exactly what we did pray. It seemed so unfair that someone who was so outgoing now stood helpless and confused within her surroundings. I knew placing my mother in a nursing home meant all hope of her returning to normal was doomed.

Chapter 8

Losing Faith

Life without my mother from a mental standpoint was becoming a reality that I just was not ready to accept or even handle. I wanted back the conversations, the hugs, the shoulder to cry on, and the encouraging words that mother's give when children are in distress. Why was this dilemma happening that made my world flip upside down more than once? I had no time to contemplate because the transition had taken on the speed of a lightning bolt striking hard and fast. The time had come to relocate my mother and it would turn out to be the most emotional day of my life. Tears flowed and my stomach was feeling like a boat that rocks back and back when the waters are rough. Sleep was inevitably and in order to focus on something other than the move I did the only thing I knew which was writing. I always found relief whenever I would write because that was the one place where I allowed myself to forget about the present. I found peace in writing my emotions on paper because it was the only way I could handle the journey of despair that had dominated my soul and captured my heart as a prisoner. The emotion that had taken residence within my body was like a volcano about to erupt. Reality had re-surfaced its ugly face and the day I dreaded to come had arrived. My sister and I escorted my mother through the doors of unfamiliar territory that would be her new home. The nurses were helpful as they appeared for the most part to be genuinely caring. We began to settle my mother into her new residence and I could not help but think this is not where she is supposed to be. All I wanted to do was take her home so we could resume our lives. Several months went by and everything appeared to be normal but sometimes things are not as they seem. The fear I had been feeling deep within my gut about nursing homes soon came to pass. I actually thought my sister and I could resume our lives now that my mother was in a licensed facility but the dream they sold us was false. Feelings of resentment once again plagued my mind because now I had to resume being a full time caregiver. My life took another spin and there was no rest for the weary. I began to question the lesson that God was trying to convey to my soul. How was I to give Him the glory out of this situation when my heart was bitter and my mouth had no words of praise to utter. My faith was wilting, my hope had long disappeared, and I could feel my emotions boiling over like hot lava from a volcano. I just wanted to throw in the towel and call it quits. I tried not to lose focus on the task at hand as I expressed my anger and frustrations to God. It was business as usual because I could not change the situation no matter how much I complained. My sister and I began our rotation for the week making sure my mother was properly cared for while in the nursing home. I tried to understand and give the staff the benefit of the doubt since there were other patients whose needs were far more critical than my mother's. I expected her to be cared for the way they would want someone to care for their mother.

My resentment turned deadly because once again why was my sister and I taking care of my mother in a facility that was suppose to give us relief. They clearly were not capable of providing any service for people afflicted with this deadly disease. Alzheimer's pierces the hearts of loved ones who are caregivers because the journey becomes so narrow you feel like the walls are caving in all around you. I tried so hard day in and out to make the journey as joyful as possible but the agony of defeat kept consuming my brain. I thought there was a little light at the end of the tunnel but darkness reared its face again within the blink of an eye. It kept surfacing just when hope seemed to be knocking at the door. I do not even know what made me think that anyone besides my sister could care for my mother the way we did. Here I was once again trying to maintain a positive attitude as the storm reared its ferocious head. What was I to do since I needed to channel my negativity into something positive? I found solace even in the midst of the turmoil just knowing that my mother was still able to feed herself, take walks, and participate in extracurricular activities with supervision. The fear I had anticipated soon faded because my presence every other day gave me the comfort I needed in order to survive this ordeal. We sent a message indirectly to the staff letting them know that my mother meant everything to us by making surprise visits to the home. I channeled my negativity into something positive by building relationships with the other patients that occupied the floor where my mother resided. It was difficult having to resume the position of caregiver full time once again because I needed a break to refuel my thoughts. My dismantled body needed nurturing from the stress of being a caregiver. The smile my mother gave as the sweet aroma from the roses brushed pass her nostrils was refreshing to see which eased the stress. The cool evening breeze that softly hit her cheeks as we sat quietly on the bench let me know that even though the mind was distant she was still able to appreciate nature. So for 11 months the process continued but somewhere in between those months I lost my mom to a confined chair and all the walks slowly diminished. I became helpless and wanted to lash out at the world for the pain I was experiencing deep within my soul. It hurt me to the core and I tried to block the anguish and frustration I was feeling out of my mind. Why was this happening? The question I asked myself often as I tried to absorb how my mother went from walking and feeding herself to a person who no longer had any interest in doing those things or even opening her eyes. I tried hard not to point any fingers and I knew the disease would progress but no explanation was good enough from anyone to explain the sudden change. It was apparent that we needed a facility that specifically handled Alzheimer patients. It was the only option or the inevitably would occur sooner than expected which was Death. My sister and I kept my mother comfortably as we began our search for a more suitable environment that focused only on patients with limited abilities association with the disease.

Chapter 9

Desperately Seeking Help

Here I was again feeling uncomfortable, angry, frustrated, and sad because something needed to take place right away. I was a ticking time bomb ready to explode at any moment and I truly wanted to make everyone hurt as much as I was hurting. I watched in distress as I tried to understand why my mother's condition had shifted downhill without any reasonable explanation from the staff or the doctors. They all kept associating the change with the disease and I was having a hard time trying to believe that was the case. I prepared myself mentally to keep doing what was best for my mother in spite of the circumstances while we continued searching for a new facility. Each day was becoming more difficult to handle and I honestly did not see any way out of the tunnel. It was as if I suddenly became blind trying to find my way through the darkness where there once was light. I became invisible as I closed my eyes and my heart not wanting to see or feel the agony that was piercing every inch of my body. The journey my sister and I were travelling was painful, humiliating, sad, and discouraging. My sister had strength and patience throughout the search and I wanted to hide where no one could find me. We continued to care for my mother even though she was unable to walk & talk as she did a month ago. I acted as if things were normal by talking to her, taking her for walks, and telling her to open your eyes because I know you want to see me. It was sad that she would never be able to do those simple things again, but I found peace in knowing that I could talk to her even if she was miles away. I believed somewhere in the darkness of the disease that a ray of sunshine existed allowing my mother to understand me whenever she heard my voice. It was difficult some days just sitting with her in silence because I had so many things I wanted to say. My mother was miles away but I always felt that she sensed my presence in the room as I reminisced about our time together on Sunday mornings in church. A part of me was envious of my sister because my mother seemed to respond to her voice more and it made me sad. My past relationship with my mother was trying to creep back into my conscious so I would feel alone as I did growing up. We received news that a bed was available and we were so delighted I almost forgot to breathe. It was the week before Christmas and I could not have asked for a better gift. God had answered our prayers and for the first time in a long time, I felt relieved, overwhelmed with joy, and grateful for the new beginning. All the issues that had taken place associated with the disease seemed so far out of my mind. The only thing that made any sense at that moment was getting my mother in the care of people who understood her world. I did not mind the move this time because it signified hope, happiness, and peace. My sister and I were never so happy the day we dressed our mother for her trip to her second new home. Out with the old in with the new was the song that played as I did a dance to the elevator out the door of the nursing home that stole my hope.

No looking back only forward as a new chapter of my life was about to begin. I had such a big smile as we entered the doors of the new facility I could not help but praise God. It was so uplifting to meet a staff whose professional mannerism was friendly and pleasant as they guided us through the floor plan used for the patients. We took a tour of my mother's living quarters, the dining room area, safety procedures, and the daily activities for the patients. The clinical team assured us that our mother was in safe hands with all state. They provided the necessities needed in caring for my mother and I no longer had to fulfill that task as I had done in the other nursing home. My sister and I were stress free and I was relieved to have some peace. I was not confident about the nursing homes agenda since similar words from the other nursing home ended in heartbreak. It took a while to adjust to the new procedures since my sister and I provided everything my mom needed towards her care. We explained the issues we encountered that made us feel uncomfortable about the promise made to care for our mother. They assured us that her well-being would always be their top priority and it was for all the patients in the nursing home. After a month of settling my mother in her new surroundings, it was refreshing to know that everything told to us happened. My mother still was unable to walk or open her eyes but I always felt she knew her surroundings. I witnessed her body jolt whenever she would hear our voices, which was something that had not happened in a long time. I felt re-energized visiting my mother in an environment where the patient's well-being was priority to a staff that was dedicated and caring. My mind was at ease and fighting sleep was no longer a battle. My mother's outer appearance was pleasing to the eyes as she always looked like a freshly cut bouquet of flowers. It was amazing to see a menu that was appealing to the stomach and succulent to the nose. The nursing home received an A+ in my book for appearance, service, and professionalism. My mother was getting the best care possible that made me happier than I had been in months. The clinical staff along with her nurses kept us updated on any changes regarding her eating habits and medical reports. They were very attentive regarding my mother's medical condition, personal appearance, and eating habits which was a relief and definitely good for our souls. I always anticipated a storm and instead my heart was overjoyed with gladness every time I saw my mother. I continued on my journey giving my mother all the love and kisses I had inside me. I thanked God for the little things in my life like touching and holding my mother's hand. Hope was in the air, which made my heart skip a beat every time my mother's eyes would flicker when I touched her hand. My mother was miles away but the story had no ending in my mind because her life still existed, and I believed anything was possible because I believed in God. Life was blossoming in spite of the darkness and I found tranquility even in the midst of silence. Visiting my mom had taken on a new meaning and while I still was feeling emotionally drained I found myself at the end of the day anxiously awaiting my next visit.

I had a different outlook on my visit experiences as I witnessed my demeanor change from resentment to appreciation. I was still able to attend to my mother's needs and I realized it was a blessing because she had life. So I continued on my perplexed journey as a caregiver thanking God every day for my mother. My visits scaled down to weekends and it felt like I was neglecting my mother even though I knew she was safe. I was relieved to know that in spite of my changes my sister's schedule remained the same for the week. We kept each other informed concerning any issues about my mother that were few since the staff had everything under control. They were not perfect but they were attentive, compassionate, professional, and caring that we really had no complaints. There were times when I did not make a weekend because I needed to be alone in my thoughts, which for a long time was not the case. Months flew by and I could see a change in my mother's desire to eat that had me concerned. Her bodily motions were becoming less, which gave me an uneasy feeling as I tried once again to understand what was happening. The sweet flavors of dessert were no longer enticing to my mother, which was the one thing she loved. I was not ready to accept her refusal to eat even if food was not appealing to her taste buds.

Chapter 10

The Journey ends

The staff always had fights over who would feed my mother because unlike the other patients she never gave any problems and she always ate everything on her tray especially the dessert. We all agreed that when food was no longer desirable to my mother it would be time to consider other options. We continued the process of attempting to feed her and some days were successful but most of the time it was a challenge just to get her to open her mouth. My mind had once again shifted to a place called denial because I realized that without food the body could not survive. The clinical staff offered options and one was to think about placing a feeding tube in my mother which was out of the question. The side effects could cause an infection or bleeding and we wanted to keep my mother comfortable not miserable. I continued on my unpredictable journey showering my mother with all the love and kisses I had left inside of me still hoping she would resume the desire to eat. My mother needed to open her mouth and I prayed to God for a miracle. I wrote a letter to my mother to ease the depression and pain that had gobbled up my body and mind. The anxiety and frustration that was bottled up inside me I released in the letter. My name and my face have drifted away to an unknown place but your love remains the same even though the words I Love You will never be expressed. Your love will forever warm my heart your love will remind me of our time spent together laughing crying talking and it's the Love I will always cherish because there is nothing greater than the love of a mother and your love will forever keep my heart and my soul smiling. This is my letter to you just to say thank you for the Sunday morning conversations which kept me sane. Thank you for the discipline when I needed it and the hugs and kisses you gave when you knew I was depressed. You can't say my name or look in my eyes but I thank God for your presence which is all the love I need right now. You may be a million miles away but I still feel love flowing from your heart to mine and that will never die. The letter gave me peace for the moment and just thinking about how my mother loved her children, grandchildren, and others took me away from reality to a place of happiness. I relied on my faith which brought me to a place of joy instead of sorrow. My sister and I continued our routine of attempting to feed my mother when we received a phone call from the doctor that would turn out to be the worst days of my life. You expect your loved ones to live forever and you are never prepared to hear any bad news. The doctor informed my sister and I that there was nothing they could do since my mother was not responding to the medicine after becoming ill. We were not ready to give up so we explored every possible outlet to keep our mother alive. The thought of her dying just was not realistic in my mind even though I knew we had done all we could for her. It was time to let go peacefully so my mother would not have to suffer any longer from this deadly disease.

I recalled being asked by the medical team if my mother would want to live with her condition or would she want to go be with her maker. I was not ready for this conversation and this time I could not pull any energy from my sister as I always did when I felt pressured. My sister was numb and I could see it in her eyes as I witnessed the tears rolling down her cheeks as we both sat speechless. We were both in a place where there was no energy to give because darkness had guzzled our mind, body, and soul. Heartbroken and helpless we urgently tried to find an alternative solution for the situation at hand. My sister and I kept our mother comfy since there was nothing else we could do but wait which was crazy when I thought about it. Watching a loved one live out their final days is the cruelest feeling in the world because you are powerless. Nothing could ever repair my broken heart as I observed my mother beginning to wither away like a flower. I was not ready to let go and I honestly can admit I was being selfish. The days seemed longer and the nights were restless as I paced the floors trying not to sleep scared the phone would ring with that fatal call. We had to begin the process of calling family members and for the first time I realized that my mother's time on earth would soon come to an end. I beckoned our pastor to come pray for my mother and our family which for me was a phone call that was to soon. I just wanted to wake up from this bad dream but unfortunately it was not a dream and I had to pull it together because I was sinking in my sorrows. My sister and I hoped for a long time to see my mother open her eyes and the night before she passed God answered our prayers. My mother opened her eyes and gave one finally look around the room at her children and grandchildren. The room was filled with joy as we uttered hello so excited as she looked at us her since her eyes had been closed for such a long time. In that moment I was so ecstatic I could not stop smiling and it felt so good to see my family shouting and clapping for joy. My mother was the back bone of our family and she kept us all on one accord, and even in her illness she kept us together as one. It was however a bitter sweet moment for my sister and I because we knew my mother would be leaving soon and for me it was to much to digest. This night would be the longest most somber one of my life and I wished for a miracle because I just was not ready to call it quits. As I departed the facility in my mind I hoped God would keep my mother until morning because I still had so much more to say to her. The walk was slow to the elevator and I wanted to stay and sleep next to my mother so I could just hold her hand all night and lay my head on her chest. I did not want her to be alone because I wanted her to know I was there in case she decided to slip away in the midnight hour. God's unchanging hand took hold of me as I slept through the night which was the first time in a while since my mother became ill. I woke up the next morning grateful that the phone did not ring and my mother would have one more day on earth.

I decided to work a half day and then head over to the facility but I told my oldest son to go be with grandma until my sister and I arrived. I began my day feeling relieved that I had another day to see my mother but as fate would have it God sent his angel on the morning of April 15,

The Journey ends

2015 to her bedside. My mother took her final breath around 10:45am with her oldest grandchild by her side. She finally was at peace but I on the other hand was traumatized and griefstricken. She was finally free from the terrible disease that had taken control of her mind for 12 long years. I tried hard to consume my tears as I made my way over to my boss's office to tell her the news. It was hard trying to get myself together for the longest drive of my life. I prayed for God to guide my hands as I drove to the facility to say my final goodbye to the woman who was my hero and protector. My long journey caring for my mother had come to an end and I was resentful, confused, angry, and emotional. I wanted it all back which was ironic since I struggled with becoming a caregiver since the day I became one. As I entered the facility the walk this time to the elevator seemed so long and far away. I franticly made my way to the second floor feeling like I was about to pass out. My heart began to beat at a rapid speed as I existed the elevator making my way to my mother's room. As I entered the room I could feel myself gasping for air as my eyes filled with water on the way to her bedside. I belted out a loud scream as I grabbed hold of her leaning on her chest for dear life asking why God why. This would be the last time I would see her, touch her, kiss her, and talk to her which caused my body to be numb. There was no joy or laughter left within my soul as I prayed to God for some peace. In my mind I did not know how I was going to keep on living without my mother in my life. I needed air so I made a mad dash for the elevator walking as fast as humanly possible to get outside so I could breathe. My mother was now in a place that we all will go to someday but my heart was crushed as I sat in silence remembering all our years together. The tears flowed down my face and I was empty, lonely, and stiff. I am still saddened by your passing and you may be physically gone but spiritually you are very much alive in me. I am constantly reminded of how wonderful you were when the mention of your name brings a smile to everyone you touched with your love. You gave of yourself unselfishly to us and others and you will forever live within our hearts. Your legacy of giving and your love for all God's people are a part and will always be a part of our

The Journey ends

---

lives always and forever. So until we meet again I Love You Mommy beyond the Moon and Stars. Sleep in Peace my Angel for your work on earth is complete.

Mommy remember me its your Daughter

www.ingramcontent.com/pod-product-compliance
Lightning Source LLC
LaVergne TN
LVHW051957060526
838201LV00059B/3693